# Old BRECHIN

*by*
Fiona Scharlau

Floods along River Street were a common occurrence, and although an embankment was completed in 1879–1880 this had little useful effect. The tenements in the street did not have a good reputation and were a byword for filthy and unsanitary conditions. Flooding must have aggravated the problem enormously, as when the waters receded they left a thick layer of mud behind them. Inhabitants lit fires to dry out their homes using coals and firewood donated by businesses in the town, or bought using money raised at special cinema performances. Ironically, the floods attracted many tourists, who came to see the spectacle. Life went on for the inhabitants of the River Street tenements, however, as this photograph of a precarious milk delivery from the Cookston Dairy illustrates.

ISBN 1 84033 134 8

With the exception of the picture on page 16, all the images in this book have been reproduced from the collection of Cultural Services. If you would like copies of any of these pictures, please contact: Angus Archives, Montrose Library, 214 High Street, Montrose, DD10 9RS, www.angus.gov.uk/history.

## FURTHER READING

The publications listed below were used by the author during her research. None of them are available from Stenlake Publishing. Those interested in finding out more are advised to contact their local bookshop or reference library.

*Brechin Advertiser*
*Old Statistical Account of Scotland*
*New Statistical Account of Scotland*
*Edwards Pocket History and Guide to Brechin*
'Vathek', *Brechin of Today*
*A Guide to Brechin Cathedral*
D. H. Edwards, *Mair Aboot It* (unpublished proof copy)
David Dakers Black, *A History of Brechin*
Brechin almanacs
Angus Archives research files

## ACKNOWLEDGEMENTS

The author extends grateful thanks to the staff of Cultural Services and Brechin Library for answering her many questions. The assistance of Amanda Pirie, Brechin Librarian, was especially appreciated.

Brechin High Street and the numerous closes running off it were home to the town's merchants and several local characters. Black Bull Close, illustrated here and named after an inn of the same name, was fairly typical. It was once the address of Provost David Doig, who had extensive business interests in Antigua and Scotland, and whose daughter Christian married into the nobility and became Lady Carnegie of Kinnaird. Another famous resident of the close was John 'Gauger' Ogilvy, an exciseman. The smuggling of whisky from the glens was once rife, and a common Gaelic prayer implored that the 'diel wad dance awa wi' the exciseman'. Ogilvy's zeal in catching law-breakers may have stemmed from his upbringing as the son of a Kirriemuir minister. It was a rare occurrence for him to be outwitted by a smuggler, but it did happen with a shipment of whisky from Edzell. He and twelve men rode to Edzell in the early hours of the morning but failed to pay attention to a funeral procession that they passed. Ogilvy later discovered that the hearse had contained the whisky barrels and the smugglers were inside the mourning coaches. The advent of regulated distilleries in the late eighteenth century heralded the end of the era of smuggling.

# INTRODUCTION

The ancient town of Brechin is situated on the banks of the River South Esk in the old county of Angus or Forfarshire. Its name is reputedly derived from the Gaelic word for a brae or hill, which aptly describes the town's location on a long sloping hill rising up from the river to beyond the High Street.

Brechin was founded upon an early Christian settlement, which was established around 1,000 years ago by King Kenneth Mac Malcolm (971–995), who gave 'the great city [of Brechin] to the Lord' and founded a church dedicated to the Holy Trinity. This was based on the Irish model of priesthood, and its members, known as Culdees, differed from their Roman Catholic successors in many ways (they were allowed to marry, for instance). Later the cathedral came under Roman Catholic rule and a bishop was installed. The bishop's burgh was granted the right to hold a weekly market and various other privileges, reflecting the cathedral's status as the 'mother church of Angus'. Over many centuries the cathedral acquired lands and wealth from patrons such as Sir Walter Stewart, Earl of Atholl and Lord of Brechin. In 1429 Stewart endowed it with lands to pay for the maintenance of a song school to train choristers.

In the eleventh century Brechin must have been a place of significance as invading Vikings found it a worthwhile target to attack. It remained an important town throughout the medieval period, but following the Reformation of the Roman Catholic Church in the 1560s the cathedral was reduced to the status of a parish church. Brechin held a weekly market for local commodities such as fish, which was brought in from Montrose. The bishop's market had formerly been held on a Sunday, but this was not considered suitable by the reformed church, and it was moved to another day. A number of fairs were also held, the most important of which was Trinity Fair, held on the town's muir.

In 1641 King Charles I reconfirmed the former Episcopal burgh's rights and privileges as a royal burgh, and despite the upheavals of the seventeenth century Brechin established a town council and began to govern its own affairs. A Guildry of Merchants was established which boosted trade both locally, and in some cases internationally. The family of Provost David Doig, who made a fortune in Antigua from their sugar plantations, were not alone in acquiring money and lands from national and international trade. Six Trades Incorporations were established, representing the hammermen, bakers, skinners, tailors, shoemakers and weavers of Brechin. These regulated trade and offered charity to 'decayed' members and their widows and orphans.

During the Jacobite Rebellion of 1715 Brechin raised an army for the Old Pretender and the burgh was taken over by Jacobite sympathisers. The town took a less active role during the 1745 rising, perhaps as a result of their earlier experiences. Smuggling and illicit distilling were also important activities in the eighteenth century.

By the late eighteenth century many new ventures had been launched, fuelled by the Industrial Revolution. Linen weaving became the largest single source of employment in the town, and was vital to the local economy. The introduction of power loom weaving concentrated production in large factories which employed many women. By the middle of the nineteenth century Brechin sustained a paper mill, two flax mills, five linen factories, two bleachfields, two distilleries, a brewery, two sawmills and two nurseries.

Industrial employment reached a peak in the 1880s and declined slowly thereafter. Despite this, Brechin continued to grow as a residential centre during the nineteenth century. Prior to then the town had remained largely within its medieval boundaries, with most Brechiners living in 2 or 3 room tenements. Between 1800 and 1850 the population grew from 4,000 to 8,000 leading to overcrowding and poor sanitary conditions. By the 1870s the town council had adopted the General Police and Improvement Act and had begun to take steps to improve public health. New streets were created, along with a public park and a new hospital. Water was piped into homes, street lighting provided and the construction of inside toilets encouraged from the late nineteenth century onwards. Other improvements, such as the building of the infirmary in 1869, were funded by private societies. During the 1950s and 1960s the work of reducing overcrowding continued, with many new houses being constructed on the outskirts of the town to relieve overcrowding. Brechin's industry received a boost during World War II with the relocation of businesses such as Coventry Gauge and Tool to the town and the setting up of an airbase at Edzell. In 1975 Brechin Town Council became part of Angus District Council, and Brechin has been under the control of Angus Council since 1996.

Brechin's High Street must be one of the steepest in Scotland. The layout of the buildings, with garden ground radiating out behind them in long thin burgage plots, reflects its medieval origins. Many of the gable ended buildings fronting the street retain the character of the seventeenth and eighteenth centuries, and until they began to move to less crowded new streets in the early nineteenth century, wealthy Brechin merchants lived here. Surviving seventeenth century merchants' houses, with their gable ends facing the street, can be seen in the right foreground. This photograph predates 1880 when the building at the top of the street housing Dickson and Turnbull, seedsmen, was demolished and replaced by the Dalhousie Hotel. The stonework and metal lamp holder in the left foreground belonged to one of the six public wells that brought fresh water into the burgh.

This view of the top half of the High Street shows the Town House, dating from 1789, to the left. Funds to build it were raised by public subscription and donations from the Guildry. The building provided accommodation for the town council, plus a courtroom, prison and a fine Guild Hall for social events. In 1833 the author of the *New Statistical Account* described it as a 'respectable edifice', although the new Town House quickly proved to be too small and was superseded in 1894 by the Municipal Buildings in Bank Street. The building to the right of the Town House once belonged to Provost John Smith; his wife was reputedly the first woman in Brechin to own a tea kettle. Latterly the house became the premises of the Brechin Baking Company, and subsequently Belford's Bakery and later Gellatly's. It is now the Bakehouse Coffee Shop, maintaining a connection with baking dating back 150 years. In front of the Town House is a Victorian cast-iron lamp-post featuring entwined fish, which marks the spot where the old market cross stood before its removal in 1767.

THE MUCKLE MARKET
BRECHIN

The High Street was the location for various markets including the Muckle Market. This was a feeing or hiring market which was held twice a year on the first Tuesday after Whit Sunday and Martinmas. Farm workers congregated near the Crown Hotel, a popular rendezvous for farmers, hoping to be given work. The market also featured a host of other attractions such as music from fiddlers, pipers and ballad singers, various showmen, plus stalls selling factory seconds from all over the country. The day after a Muckle Market was called Little Wednesday, a reference, no doubt, to the lack of work that was accomplished.

A busy Muckle Market showing the High Street taken up with stalls and carts selling all manner of goods. The lamp-post marking the site of the old market cross is being used as a convenient prop for holding up a mountain of chairs.

The lower half of the High Street has a quieter character with fewer shops. During the 1920s the projecting whitewashed building with its gable end to the street was demolished to allow the road to be widened and the King's cinema to be built. The late eighteenth and early nineteenth centuries saw a great deal of improvement work take place in the burgh's most important street. Projecting forestairs and gables were removed, the market cross was taken down to ease the flow of traffic, and a grand new Town House was erected on the site of the medieval tolbooth. The steep street was terraced until the various different levels were filled in to create a smooth hill, and it was macadamised under the Municipal Reform Act of 1838.

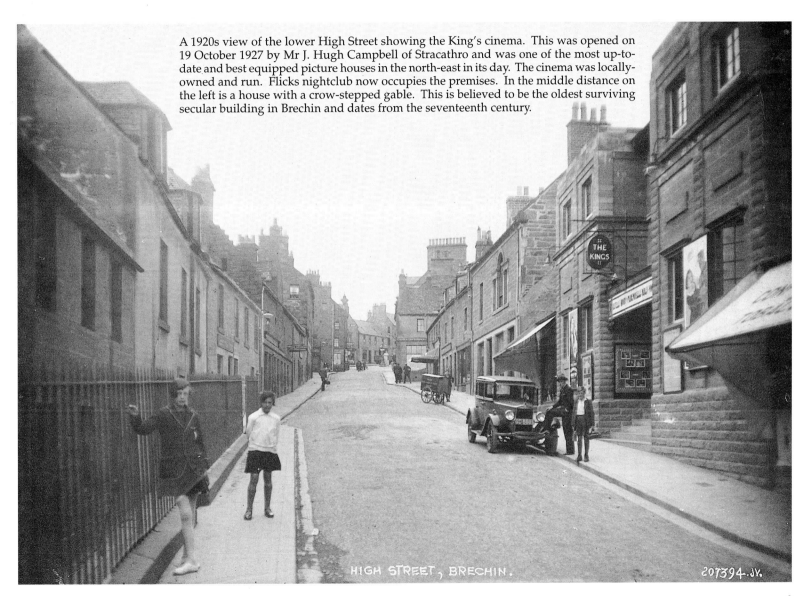

A 1920s view of the lower High Street showing the King's cinema. This was opened on 19 October 1927 by Mr J. Hugh Campbell of Stracathro and was one of the most up-to-date and best equipped picture houses in the north-east in its day. The cinema was locally-owned and run. Flicks nightclub now occupies the premises. In the middle distance on the left is a house with a crow-stepped gable. This is believed to be the oldest surviving secular building in Brechin and dates from the seventeenth century.

HIGH STREET, BRECHIN.

207394.JV.

An unusual view of the back of the High Street or Back Braes as seen from the Skinner's Burn area. The burn's name is derived from the skinners and tanners who once had their pits at its side. The last known tanning business in the town was the Ford Mouth Tannery run by Provost John Molison and partners in the late eighteenth century. This view of the Back Braes shows an interesting roofline and illustrates that houses on the lower High Street are often twice as tall at the rear as they appear from the street.

On Christmas Day 1906 a severe snowstorm began. It lasted nearly a week, and heavily drifting snow left Brechin completely isolated, with telephone and telegraph wires brought down by the weight of the snow. Businesses ground to a virtual standstill as the snow fell faster than the streets could be cleared, and shopkeepers found themselves unable to deliver goods for the New Year festivities. While adults must have found the situation trying, the children of Brechin viewed it as an opportunity for fun. Children of all ages and eras have always enjoyed playing in the snow, and these ones in Church Street were no exception.

Church Street during the severe Christmas snowstorms of 1906. The street follows the north edge of the old Chanonry district where the officials of the cathedral once had their houses and gardens. After the Reformation these properties were gradually sold off by the town council to individuals who were prepared to rescue them from the ruinous state into which they had fallen. In the eighteenth century Church Street became a fashionable location for the winter homes of members of the aristocracy such as Lady Ballownie. The tower of the Brechin Mechanics Institute is visible at the far end of the street.

The Mechanics Institute was intended to rehouse Brechin's burgh, parish and grammar schools in a suitable modern building. It was designed by John Henderson of Edinburgh, who had been born in Brechin the son of the Earl of Dalhousie's gardener. The foundation stone was laid on 28 June 1838, the day of Queen Victoria's Coronation, and the building was regarded as a great ornament to the west end of the town. It has served a number of other purposes over the years including providing a reading room, a wartime billet for soldiers, an artist's studio for David Waterson, an art gallery and a home for the Brechin Guildry. This photograph was taken after 1897 when the Dalhousie Fountain – in memory of Fox Maule Ramsay – was relocated from in front of the institute to St Ninian's Square.

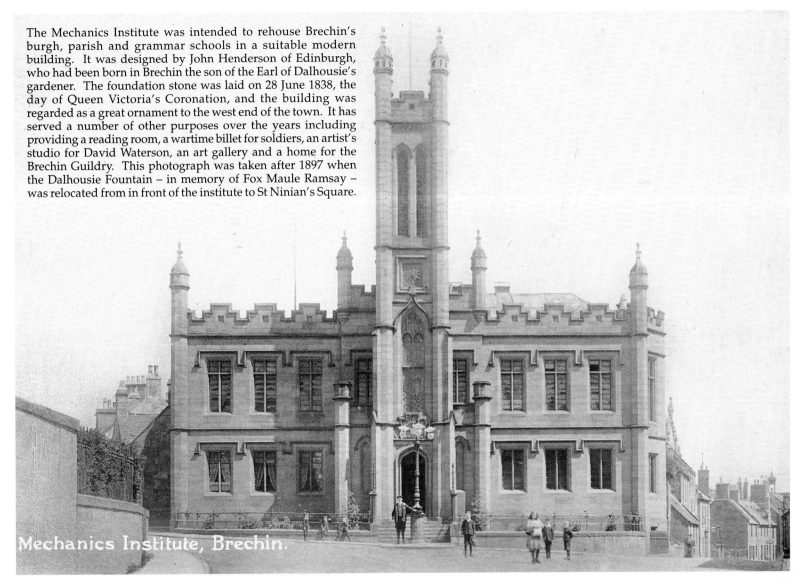

Mechanics Institute, Brechin.

These quaint eighteenth century weavers' houses on Cadger Hillock, now Montrose Street, were nicknamed the Benches after the warping and winding benches used in the buildings. Anyone passing by outside would have been able to clearly hear the sound of the shuttles as the handloom weavers sat working at their webs while their wives and children spun and provided the pirns. Weaving in Brechin expanded greatly in the late eighteenth and early nineteenth centuries. In 1833, when the Brechin entry of the *New Statistical Account* was written, between 1,000 and 1,500 people were employed as weavers. This number grew as the century progressed. By the middle of the nineteenth century, however, the trend was towards building factories to house the new power looms. In 1863 the old Benches were cleared away to make room for R. & D. Duke's new factory, the Denburn Linen Works.

The annual market at Trinity (pronounced Taranty) Muir had a county-wide reputation. In the nineteenth century it was a huge week-long event for the selling or bartering of sheep, cattle and horses. It also had a recreational side with stalls and sideshows, and was well attended by gypsies and dealers as well as farmers, farm servants and their girlfriends, showmen and townsfolk. The town's magistrates had a presence too, and operated a court to punish wrongdoers immediately. Town officials carried their halberts to enforce magistrates' decisions, and were aided by representatives sent by each of the town's incorporated trades. The fair began to fall into decline with the rise of regular auction marts. It was initially reduced to a three-day event, and then cut to a single day at the beginning of the twentieth century, when the recreational side began to assume greater importance with boxing stalls, ice cream barrows, displays of agricultural machinery and fortune tellers.

Swan Street was named after the Swan Inn, which was demolished in 1863 to allow the road to be widened. This was one of the main arteries used by the *Defiance* stagecoach as it travelled through the town en route to Aberdeen and Edinburgh – not to mention for country carts bringing produce to market. The *Defiance* was instituted in 1829 and covered the 129 miles from Aberdeen to Edinburgh in 12 hours. It could accommodate four people sitting inside and eleven sitting outside, and left the Swan Inn at 11 a.m., arriving in Edinburgh about 8.30 p.m. Joseph C. Robertson, whose house and draper's shop were at 98 High Street, is seen here feeding the pigeons in Swan Street.

ST. DAVID STREET, BRECHIN

St David Street, formerly Upper Wynd, was little more than a muddy lane until improvements were made in the early 1800s. It originally formed a path along the boundary of the old medieval burgh limits, but by the late nineteenth and early twentieth centuries had become a thriving shopping street. In 1882 the post office moved there, with its new premises a vast improvement on the 'dingy little apartment' it had previously occupied in Church Street. At this time it was still possible for the mail carrier to carry the entire post between Brechin and Montrose in his hat. St David Street is still a busy shopping street today.

St. David Street, Brechin.

The large Victorian building on the left-hand corner at the junction of St David Street and the High Street was built on the site of the house and shop affectionately known as the Auld Neuk House. This was the property of the Guthrie family, who in the late eighteenth and early nineteenth centuries provided Brechin with a number of provosts, merchants and bankers. It was also the birthplace of Dr Thomas Guthrie, the philanthropist who founded the Ragged Schools in Edinburgh.

The South Port, at the junction of Bridge Street (to the right) and Union Street (to the left), was formerly the site of gates controlling access to the town from this direction. Merchants bringing in goods for market day would have to stop at these gates and pay the petty customs due on their items before they could proceed. Some burghs had purpose-built town walls, while others relied on the walls or ditches at the rear of properties to offer protection. The South Port was pulled down in 1759 when it had become an impediment to the growing volume of traffic, and this photograph was taken in the winter of 1906. The South Port Bar once looked straight up the High Street.

River Street has been entirely redeveloped over the past century. Once known as Nether Tenements of Caldhame, it originally lay outside the burgh boundary and was a favourite place for merchants and tradesmen to live and work, being beyond the rules and regulations of the Trades Incorporations and the Guildry of Merchants. The town council set about improving the area in the 1880s with money bequeathed for improvement work by the Reverend George Alexander. A row of hovels was demolished *c*.1879–1880 to create a pretty riverside walk. Other properties were given to the town for the express purpose of demolition. Railings were erected after 1884 by Provost Duncan to prevent children from falling into the river.

The North Port Distillery was founded around 1820 by the firm of Guthrie, Martin & Co. Ltd. By the 1860s it was producing over 70,000 gallons of whisky annually and employed 25 men at 14 shillings per week. The distillery's brand was popular in the leading hotels of London, Glasgow and Edinburgh. In 1983 the North Port Distillery went out of business after which its buildings were demolished to make way for a supermarket.

West Toll, Brechin. Tollhouses were in use between the late eighteenth century and 1879 when toll roads were abolished. They were occupied by speculators who bid for the right to collect tolls and often sold alcohol from their tollhouses too. The tollhouse is still occupied as a family home.

Brechin owes its existence to the Celtic church which developed into the medieval cathedral dedicated to the Holy Trinity. The earliest surviving part of the cathedral is the tenth century round tower, one of only two in Scotland (the other being in Abernethy). When King David I reformed the Celtic church the cathedral was transformed into a bishopric and consequently grew in importance. It became the mother church of Angus and the Mearns, but its influence came to an end after the Reformation during the 1560s when bishops and the Catholic Church were swept away. It assumed a new role as the parish church of Brechin which it fulfils to this day.

The fabric of the cathedral remained largely untouched until an unsympathetic restoration project in 1807 destroyed much of its medieval character. The stalls and trades lofts which had grown in an ad hoc fashion were removed, and lines of pews were installed. This restoration was later described as an act of vandalism. A second and more appropriate restoration programme was undertaken in 1900–1901 under the guidance of Keppie and Honeyman, a firm of Glasgow architects which then employed Charles Rennie Macintosh. This photograph shows some of the men involved in the restoration project.

The Den was originally well outside the burgh boundaries and its extensive lands provided pasture for the burgesses' cows and horses. They paid a herd to take their animals out to pasture on a daily basis. By the beginning of the nineteenth century few burgesses were taking advantage of this right, and in 1812 the Den was rouped to John Henderson, who converted it into a nursery. It was used for this purpose for over a century. Henderson sold forest and fruit trees as well as ornamental shrubs and bushes.

The part of the Den in front of Henderson's nursery was acquired by the Parochial Board in 1856 for a new burial ground. The town council granted permission to build a bridge over the Den to provide access to the site. Ground was also made available to build an infirmary for Brechin, which originally only treated infectious diseases. The former St Columba's church, in the background, is now an interior decorator's showroom.

Brechin's public park was gifted to the town by Lord Dalhousie in 1867 and was further enlarged to celebrate Queen Victoria's Golden Jubilee. The park featured the beautiful cast iron bandstand shown in this photograph, as well as drinking wells, a skating pond, an ornamental pool, space for playing football and a bowling green. Until the Second World War it was also home to a cannon from the Crimean War. It was said that on Wednesdays the park was full of shopkeepers, with factory workers going there on Sundays (reflecting their respective days off), and it was always crowded. Cricket was a popular pastime amongst the boys of the burgh, who formed teams or 'clubbies', and would go around houses or stop people in the street to ask for money to buy cricket equipment for their team. The clubbies had interesting names such as the Defiant, the Orion and I Zingari.

Brechin, in common with other Scottish burghs, played host to a variety of markets and fairs. Tuesday was the regular day for the grain market, and during the autumn and winter sales of cattle also took place on Tuesdays. A weekly horse market was held in February and March. As well as the famous Trinity Fair, Trinity Muir hosted a variety of other markets. This photograph shows Term Market in St Ninian's Square (the market previously took place in the High Street). In the final years of the nineteenth century the square was gentrified with the addition of the Gothic-style Gardner Memorial Church and the building of the public library between 1891 and 1893.

The formation of Brechin Operatic Society reflected the growth in leisure pursuits in the town from the mid-nineteenth century onwards. Sporting, social and recreational societies of all kinds developed and flourished during this period. In 1839 a horticultural society was established, with a cricket club following in 1849 and a bowling club in 1862. Musical societies of all types grew from the middle class tradition of holding musical soirees and private subscription balls.

THE GREAT FLOODS AT BRECHIN MAY 9th 1913

The rainstorms of 1913, during which Brechin and the north-east suffered a week of torrential rain and hurricane-force winds, were unprecedented. The South Esk was soon in spate and River Street tenants prepared for the inevitable with sandbags, although they could do little to prevent the worst flood in 40 years from sweeping into their homes to a depth of three or four feet. Those who could not find a friend or relative to take them in until the waters receded were given shelter at the almshouse or in the Town Hall. The area was submerged for 30 hours before water levels began to fall.

St Ninian's Square was converted to gardens in 1897. Previously it had been the site of the old slaughterhouse and a favourite spot for travelling shows, as well as meetings of Chartists and a venue for other orators. It also provided housewives with a washing green. This picture of the square shows the tank *Julian* on a Scotland-wide fund-raising tour during the First World War. Brechin's provost and other officials are perched on the top of the tank with the town officer standing guard below them.

Brechin was one of the last burghs to maintain the ancient tradition of riding the marches. Once a year the magistrates and their invited guests would assemble at the market cross in their best clothes. From there, attended by the town officer and drummer, the party would set off on a tour of the burgh's boundaries to ensure that all the rights of way were clear and that no illegal fences had been erected. By the twentieth century this exercise had become largely ceremonial and instead of riding on horseback the party would walk or be driven. As this photograph shows, on occasion the ceremony did still play a role in ensuring that burgh lands were not encroached upon. The town officer, watched by the magistrates, is cutting an illegal fence to re-establish the correct boundary markers.

One of the duties of the councillors was to make an annual inspection of the town's water supply. Brechin had a reliable source of water from the mid-eighteenth century, when the council purchased the Dove Wells of Cookston and piped a supply from there to six public wells. Piped water into individual houses and buildings was available from 1839 on payment of water rates. From the 1870s, however, Brechin obtained its supply from the Mooran Water. This scheme extended the provision of water to a greater number of Brechiners by providing 300,000 gallons per day. Once a year the councillors made the trip to the Mooran Water where they had a picnic lunch and checked the quality of the water.

An unidentified councillor checking the water quality.

Councillors enjoying an afternoon nap after testing the waters of the Mooran.

The tradition of proclaiming the accession of a new monarch at the site of the market cross is an ancient one. This picture shows the proclamation of the short reign of Edward VIII being made by Town Clerk Fred Ferguson, attended by Provost John M. Dunn (to the left of the clerk, wearing the fur collar). The town officer is also in attendance, standing below the platform and carrying his ceremonial halbert, while the policeman at the lower right-hand corner is also carrying a halbert. A number of small children have positioned themselves at the front for a good view of the proceedings.

The current facade of Brechin railway station was built in 1896–1897 at a cost of £8,000 and replaced an earlier 'dismal, smoke begrimed place'. The Forfar and Brechin Railway opened to passenger traffic on 1 June 1895 at 7.30 a.m. The first train was decorated with flags and watched by a large crowd. Here, two boys are seen playing in a fountain in St Ninian's Square with the station buildings in the background. The photograph was taken before the booking office was built. The fountain is no longer in the square.

*Right:* A diesel train leaving Brechin station on its way to Bridge of Dun, *c.*1950s. Diesel locomotives still run on this line, which is now operated by the Caledonian Railway. The railway has preserved the four mile stretch of line, and runs a collection of steam and diesel trains during the summer and on special occasions.

Railway lines were kept open for the first two days of the 1906 snowstorm despite heavy drifting, with only slight delays while the snowploughs cleared the lines. There were few incidents, although the 6.05 p.m. from Brechin to Forfar went off the rails near Forfar station and its passengers had to get out and complete their journey on foot. By the third day of the storm the drifting snow had become so severe that the railway lines closed. The Bridge of Dun line was only reopened at midday after a great deal of effort, and this photograph was taken at Bridge of Dun after a train had completed the difficult journey from Brechin.

A passenger train arriving at Bridge of Dun after the Christmas 1906 storms.

Almost every street in Brechin was decorated with bunting and flags for the Coronation of King George VI and Queen Elizabeth on 12 May 1937. The town celebrated the event with a programme of activities that included a procession to the cathedral for a special service and an afternoon of choir performances, country dancing, boxing and wrestling, a parade of decorated motor vehicles and a fancy dress competition at the public park. The evening was rounded off by a torchlight procession, a bonfire and a midnight dance. This picture shows Mrs Graham and Mrs Munro standing outside a decorated home on Bridge Street.

Jimmy Sinclair, better known as Jimmy the Badger, was a linen handloom weaver who worked from his home in Bridge Street for John Dakers.

John Dakers established his weaving business in the Nether Tenements of Caldhame in the early nineteenth century, before moving to the top of Little Mill Stairs where they join the High Street.  When power looms became available, the business started to use them, while also retaining a number of linen handlooms.  Smart's and Duke's weaving factories also ran power and handlooms in tandem.  This view inside Dakers' weaving factory shows the last of the old handlooms.

The Inch had functioned as a public bleaching green since 1616 and became a busy industrial site during the eighteenth century when the town council let it to a commercial linen bleacher. A paper mill was established there in 1852. By the end of the nineteenth century this was producing 18,000 miles of paper every year, although the floods of the early twentieth century frequently caused a loss of production at the mill. In 1839 the Inch Bleachfield employed 40 men and 30 women, while in the same year a spinning mill on the Inch employed 22 hecklers and 40 spinners. From 1833 the Inch also housed a public wash house, a useful aid to public health in the days before houses had running water and bathrooms.

It wasn't just houses that were decorated for the Coronation of 12 May 1937, but factories and shops too. J. & J. Smart's weaving factory was no exception. Smart's was founded in 1854 with a modest number of power looms and a staff of 140 handloom weavers. By 1864 the firm was operating 308 power looms, a significant number, but still short of Duke's 500 looms at the new Denburn works. One of the company's founders, James Smart, was a well-known benefactor. He gave money to causes such as Brechin Infirmary and missions of the United Presbyterian Church, also founding a bursary in mechanical engineering at University College, Dundee.

Robert and David Duke established their weaving business in 1852, and the Denburn Works were built for them in 1864 on the site of the old Benches on Cadger Hillock (see page 14). The factory, with its tower and 200 foot facade, is arguably the finest industrial building in Brechin. In its heyday Duke's employed 800 workers on 500 power looms, and remained in the hands of the Duke family until ceasing production in 1982. Following closure the factory building was converted into residential accommodation.

On 8 July 1935 David Duke junior celebrated his golden wedding anniversary. He was greatly respected by his workforce, who decorated the factory for an open day to celebrate the occasion. The ceilings and looms were decked with miles of paper chains and streamers, along with bells, flags, bunting, artificial flowers, horseshoes and balloons. Visitors were so keen to see the decorated factory that the queue stretched up Southesk Street and along Montrose Street. The workers presented the Dukes with a massive silver rose bowl, and as a gesture of his appreciation David Duke gave his employees a day off with full pay.

James Barrie's store on Clerk Street was home to the kind of wide-ranging local business that was once to be found on the high street of almost every town. Barrie's was a combined house furnishers, auctioneers, antique dealers, valuers and appraisers. This postcard was used to send information to customers. Larger, departmentalised shops such as this one came to the fore in the late Victorian era, rivalling the plethora of small individual shops that had been dominant prior to then.

44

The Cross Keys Bakery was located in the close of the same name. This in turn was named after the Cross Keys Inn and provided access to a common bakehouse where local people could have their bread and pies baked. The tradition of baking in the close was retained by this bakery into the twentieth century.

This photograph of Bridgend Quarry near Brechin Bridge was entered in the Brechin Photographic Exhibition of *c.*1888. The quarry was one of a number in the immediate vicinity working freestone and limestone. The Bridgend area was outside the burgh boundaries and centred around the ancient bridge over the South Esk. A brewery operated in the area until at least the 1830s, and Brigend House was once the home of local artist David Waterson, who worked in the vicinity in the early to middle part of the twentieth century.

This old house in the Chanonry was known to generations of Brechiners as the Schoolie. Following the Reformation it provided a home for the grammar school for 250 years until the opening of the Mechanics Institute in 1838. Despite the cramped surroundings the schoolmaster endeavoured to teach boys Latin and prepare them for a university education. They worked long hours. In the summer, school was in session from 6 a.m. to 6 p.m. with only an hour's break. The grammar school grew out of the old cathedral song school, which was established in 1429 and trained choristers, as well as teaching them Latin.

BRECHIN HIGH SCHOOL.

Brechin's high school was erected in 1877 and provided more spacious accommodation for pupils and teachers than had been available in the Mechanics Institute. The various disciplines taught in the old burgh, parish and grammar schools were combined in the new school. When the current secondary school opened in October 1970 the old high school became Maisondieu Primary School.